SOUTHEND-ON-SEA
PAST & PRESENT

BRITAIN IN OLD PHOTOGRAPHS

SOUTHEND-ON-SEA
PAST & PRESENT

KEN CROWE

SUTTON PUBLISHING

Sutton Publishing Limited
Phoenix Mill · Thrupp · Stroud
Gloucestershire · GL5 2BU

First published 2000

Reprinted 2005

British Library Cataloguing in Publication Data
A catalogue record for this book is available from the
British Library.

ISBN 0-7509-1900-0

Half title page photograph: Garon's Tea Bar
(see p. 34)

Title page photograph: Clifftown
Congregational Church (see p. 58)

Typeset in 10.5/13.5 Photina.
Typesetting and origination by
Sutton Publishing Limited.
Printed in Great Britain by
J.H. Haynes & Co. Ltd, Sparkford.

 ## Southend Musuems Service

The service was formed in 1974, following Local Government reorganisation, and comprises the Central Museum and Planetarium, Prittlewell Priory, the Beecroft Art Gallery and Southchurch Hall. Prittlewell Priory and Southchurch Hall are both Grade I listed buildings, which were converted to museum use in 1917–21 and 1974 respectively.

Serving the people of Southend, the museums collect, among other things, material relating to the history of the Borough of Southend-on-Sea and the surrounding area. Together with important collections relating to the natural and human history of south-east Essex, the museum has a very large pictorial archive which dates from about 1790, and includes original paintings, prints and photographs. This archive is constantly being added to, and the museums service is always willing to accept donations of pictures. It also welcomes the opportunity to copy images to add to the archive, which is actively consulted by the public – researchers, general public and students – and is often drawn on for local history displays and publications such as this.

In January 1999 the Museums Service was awarded a grant from the Heritage Lottery Millennium Festival Fund, for the creation of the Southend Discovery Centre. The purpose of the Centre is to give greater public access to the Museum's collections, and will include a database of the Museum's pictorial archive. The other elements comprise Discovery Tables relating to various themes, Topic Trays for use with video microscopes, and handling collections.

Supporting the work of the museums, and promoting their use by the public, are the Friends of Southend's Museums, formed in 1983. The Friends are a major fundraising body, and important supporters of the Southend Discovery Centre. Their social and fundraising activities continue to enable the museums to increase the range and quality of services to the people of Southend.

CONTENTS

INTRODUCTION

In this book we shall be looking at the story of Southend over the past 130 years. The starting date, although not chosen for any historical reason, happens to coincide with the earliest available photographs of the area, and also with the beginnings of Southend as a holiday resort, approximating to the modern conception of a tourist destination. While Southend as we now know it was very much a product of the late eighteenth and, principally, of the second half of the nineteenth century, its origins go back in time into the later middle ages.

The origins of 'Southend' are inextricably bound up with the foundations of Prittlewell Priory in the twelfth century, by one of the county's greatest magnates, Robert fitzSuen of Essex. His grandfather was one fitzWimarc, who was well known to both Edward the Confessor and to Duke William of Normandy. With the base of his estates at Rayleigh in Essex, fitzWimarc and his son, Suen, were well placed to control their vast estates which comprised the 'Honour' of Rayleigh. It was here that, to secure those lands, Suen built his castle in about 1070. Suen's son, Robert, like many of his contemporaries, was concerned to secure the everlasting salvation of his, and his family's souls, through the granting of land for the foundation of a monastery. At this time one of the most favoured orders in Europe was the Cluniacs. Thus it was that Robert fitzSuen's grant was for the foundation of a Priory, to the north-east of the small town of Prittlewell, on the north bank of the Thames.

Like all such foundations, the Priory was endowed with much other property, the income from which supported the monks and allowed them to erect and extend their buildings. This land included an area of farmland and marsh to the south, between a lane on the west which led down to the sea and a landing-stage, and the manor of Southchurch Hall on the east. It was this area of land, a few farms, a common and, along the shore, several fish traps, which became known as Southend. Gradually, from the seventeenth century onwards, settlement extended to the west, along the shore, and, by the middle of the eighteenth century, a substantial number of buildings had been erected along the north bank of the Thames towards the high cliffs to the west. Towards the end of the eighteenth century the cliff top was developed and, towards the middle of the nineteenth century, first the pier was built and then the railway came. But these are matters which will be more fully explored later in this book.

This book is very much a series of snapshots in time; it cannot be, nor does it pretend to be, a history of Southend. That has still to be written. Photographs, like any other medium of communication, carry with them the bias of the photographer. The photographer will have chosen to take a particular view, rather than another; sometimes the reasons for the choice may be, or seem to be, obvious; at other times not so. Added to this, of course, there is the undeniable bias of the author, whose job was to select which of the many thousands of photographs available to use in this work. To a not inconsiderable extent, this choice is a pragmatic one. Once the decision to illustrate certain parts of the town has been made (another bias), one then has to choose those images which can be replicated today, while also trying to avoid using too many which have been seen in other publications. For these reasons, some very fine photographs could not be used here.

This work is arranged in a form of journey, geographical and, to an extent, chronological. Starting with the oldest part of Southend – Prittlewell – we work our way down Victoria Avenue and into the town centre. Then we look at High Street and its environs. We then take a journey to the west, then to the pier and, finally, to the east.

The large majority of the photographs in this book are taken from the collections of Southend Museums. In particular they are from the Padgett and Dawson collections. Alfred Padgett worked in London, but moved to Leigh-on-Sea with his family in about 1905 to convert his hobby as a photographer into a business. His earliest photographs were taken (all on glass plates) during his visits to Southend and Leigh on holiday in the later 1890s, but the majority date from about 1905 to about 1930. During this time he worked from his home in Leigh, converting a large garden shed into his 'Haven Studios'. George Dawson was a professional chemist and, like many chemists, he supplied both amateur and professional photographers with their supplies. And like some others in his business, he also tried his hand at photography. Unfortunately we do not know when he began, or ceased, his photographic career. In the collections of Southend Museum are about 200 quarter plate negatives, all carefully numbered and dated to between 1899 and 1901. It would be most interesting to know the whereabouts of other negatives by George Dawson, and also of any surviving photographs by Southend's earliest professional photographers – Ephraim Lawton and Frank Henry Secourable.

Other photographs from the Southend Museums collections used in this work include some from the Goodale Collection, principally photographs of bomb damage of the Second World War. We are very grateful to *Evening Echo* Newspapers (who retain the copyright) for permission to use these here. We would also like to thank the owners of other collections who have allowed us to reproduce their photographs here. These include Essex Record Office, Southend Library and Southend Borough Council Engineers Department, together with the late W. Wren, Janet Purdy (for a photograph from the Jessie K. Payne collection) and John Kennedy Melling for photographs from the Noakes Collection.

A major initiative at Southend Museum currently under way is the creation of the Southend Discovery Centre at the Central Museum. The purpose behind the creation of the Centre is to enable greater public access to the collections of the Museums Service. One part of this involves the digitising of the Museum's extensive photographic archive. This will result in, eventually, all of the Musuem's photographic archive being available to the public on computer terminals. Since this will take several years to complete, the digitising will be done in stages, so that, by July of 2000, when the Centre opens, there will be about 2,000 images available. We hope to add about 1,000 or so each year. This work shall continue until all of the Museum's historic photographs (plus other subjects – local wildlife, archaeological, etc.), a total of some 15,000 or so, have been scanned into the database.

The creation of the Southend Discovery Centre has been possible only with a grant from the Millennium Festival Fund (part of the National Lottery), with partnership funding from the Museum's supporting charity, the Friends of Southend Museum. I am delighted, therefore, to be able to repay, in a very small measure, the help which my colleagues and I have received from the 'Friends'. Thus, a substantial proportion of the royalties from the sale of this book are being donated to that organisation.

The collecting, safe-keeping, restoring and eventual publication – in whatever form – of historic photographs is a vital element of our work. It is the preservation of our local, and national, heritage in a form which is immediately and uniquely accessible, but if lost or destroyed without record, is irreplaceable. I would therefore encourage anyone who has original local historic photographs to allow them to be copied by, or to donate them to, a local repository, be it a museum, library or record office, and to give as much information as possible about the scene, its date, the photographer, and so on. In this way these images, vital for a visual history of an area, will be secured for the future.

CHAPTER ONE

PRITTLEWELL AND
VICTORIA AVENUE

Although Prittlewell now forms the northern part of Southend, it is, in fact, one of
the oldest parts of that town. The area we now know as Southend comprised, in
the earlier middle ages, two manors – Prittlewell and Milton Hall. From Prittlewell
itself were created the manors of Priors or Prittlewell Priory, and Earls Hall, and a sub-
manor of Milton was also created, called Chalkwell Hall. All these areas were
encompassed within the ancient parish of Prittlewell.

The centre of the parish was the church of St Mary's, standing at the corner of East
Street and North Street, with West Street leading down to the centre of the manor of
Milton Hall to the west. The lands belonging to the Priory included the parish church,
but very little of the village itself, this remaining within the manor of Earls Hall. The life
of the village, then, revolved around the church and, to a certain extent, the Priory (the
private owners of the Priory from 1536 were also Lords of the Manor), with all the major
houses being around the crossroads. No road leading directly to the south existed before
the late nineteenth century.

These major buildings included Reynolds and Roots Hall in West Street; the former
with a huge fifteenth-century fireplace which is now displayed in Southend's Central
Museum. A similar fireplace was discovered during the demolition of another large house
in East Street, on the south side of the churchyard. Recently the village's market house
appears to have been identified, on the corner of West Street and North Street, until 1998
used as a bakers'. Also in North Street was a charity school, founded by the Lord of the
Manor in the early eighteenth century.

As may be evident from the name, Victoria Avenue, leading into the town centre from the
north, was created in the late nineteenth century. The first suggestions for a new road to link
the old Whitegate Corner with Prittlewell Church had been made in 1883. The Chairman of
the Local Board thought that the new road would be 'a great thing for both Prittlewell and
Southend, as it would complete a perfect line through High Street to Prittlewell' and that the
'direct road to Prittlewell will be one of the most important improvements to the town'. At
the same time discussions were taking place with the Great Eastern Railway Co. regarding
the route of the proposed rail link to Wickford and the site of the station at Southend. From
the late 1880s the Southend Local Board (and then the Council) began to apportion building
plots along the route of the new road, of 50 ft frontages. In 1887 a letter of complaint in the
Southend Standard suggested that the Board was being extravagant to enter into such a 'very
doubtful speculation at the cost and risk of the ratepayers of this district'.

Prittlewell Priory, 1898. The Priory, originally a Cluniac foundation dating to the twelfth century, had been a private house since 1536, when the lesser monastic houses were dissolved on the orders of Henry VIII. At the end of the nineteenth century the owners were the Scratton family (who were lords of the manor also), which family had been in residence since about 1670. Notice the large number of chimney-stacks which indicate the presence of bedrooms that had been created on floors inserted into the Prior's Chamber and Refectory. (*Reproduced by kind permission of Southend Museums*)

Today Prittlewell Priory is one of Southend's museums. The grounds and house were given to the town in 1917 by R.A. Jones, a local jeweller, who saved the property from being demolished for a housing estate. The Priory was restored, inserted floors removed, and converted for museum use. (*Author*)

Prittlewell Hill, North Street, at the northern end of Prittlewell village, photographed by George Dawson in 1900. On the left of the photograph can be seen Glynd's Charity School (second building from the left), with the tower of St Mary's church just behind. Glynd's charity school was established by the Lord of the Manor of Prittlewell, Daniel Scratton, and Thomas Case in 1727, for the education of ten poor children (originally only boys) of the parish. To the left (east) was Prittlewell Priory and to the right of the road was Earls Hall, the two ancient manor houses of Prittlewell. (*Reproduced by kind permission of Southend Museums*)

Now a dual carriageway, Victoria Avenue is the main road leading into Southend from the A127 (Southend arterial road). Glynd's charity school building and the weatherboarded cottage to the north have long disappeared, but the brick cottages to the south beyond the site of Glynd's remain. (*Author*)

Prittlewell Bridge to the north of the village, with the weatherboarded cottage, *c*. 1900. To the right of the picture are the grounds of Prittlewell Priory. The road led northwards to Cuckoo Corner (named after a family who owned the land). This is another picture taken by George Dawson of Southend.(*Reproduced by kind permission of Southend Museums*)

The same view today shows that the brick house in the middle distance is the only survivor from a century ago. The 'bridge' has long gone, and the Prittle Brook is now tunnelled below a flat road. The gates leading to Prittlewell Priory can be seen on the right. (*Author*)

This fascinating view of North Street, Prittlewell, in about 1880, looks north from the junction with East and West Streets. At this time there was no Victoria Avenue linking the village with Southend, and the only route to that modern town was via the original medieval roads. This view shows that at this date (and in fact largely until the 1930s) both sides of the road were crammed with medieval and later buildings. The buildings on the right are in front of the parish church of St Mary's. (*Reproduced by kind permission of Southend Museums*)

Another view, of approximately the same date, taken from slightly further to the east, and with a clearer view of the west side of the street. (*Reproduced by kind permission of Southend Museums*)

Today just two of the medieval buildings in Prittlewell survive, both on the west (left) side of North Street, opposite the church. Prittlewell is now just the northern suburb of the modern town of Southend. (*Author*)

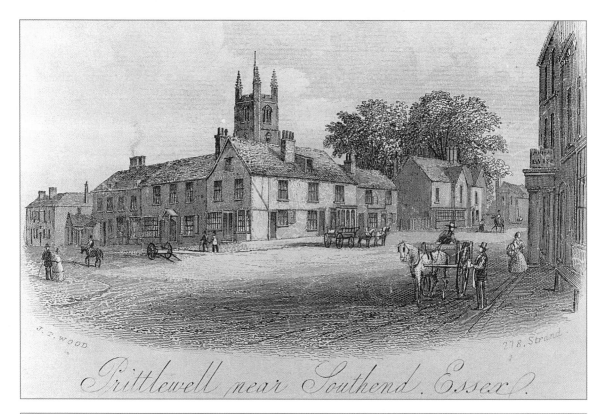

Prittlewell near Southend, Essex.

Opposite, top: An engraving of about 1870, showing the corner of East Street and North Street. Looking down East Street, we can see the large medieval house which was probably the priest's house, and which may have been the home of the Jesus Guild. (*Reproduced by kind permission of Southend Libraries*)

Opposite, below: Prittlewell village, showing the church hidden behind houses fronting East Street and North Street, *c.* 1920. Some of these houses were medieval in date, having been erected at a time when Prittlewell was a small but substantial market town. These houses were built on what was probably part of the churchyard, and some may have been connnected originally with structures used by Mystery Players. (*Reproduced by kind permission of Southend Museums*)

Today all but two of the houses have been demolished. They were pulled down in 1935, following the Prittlewell Improvement Scheme of 1912. Canon Gowing, vicar of Prittlewell from 1917, wished that people should have a clear view of his church and was keen to promote the demolition of these properties. Such action has left us determined to preserve what does remain of the medieval centre of Prittlewell. (*Author*)

These cottages were erected in 1786 on land belonging to the Lord of the Manor, near Polstead Wick, at the site which Philip Benton, in his *History of the Rochford Hundred*, tells us was called the 'three-wont-way'. This was the Workhouse – the inmates, from 1813, wearing a uniform bearing a large letter 'P' to signify that they were paupers. They were employed in spinning and weaving. The small brick building to the right was the 'lock-up', a form of punishment cell for intransigent paupers. (*Reproduced by kind permission of Southend Museums*)

When the Poor Law Union was formed in 1834, the paupers were sent to the Union Workhouse at Rochford (which eventually formed the core of Rochford Hospital), and the cottages became private houses. They were demolished in about 1960, and on their site now are blocks of flats. (*Author*)

Oaken Grange Drive in Prittlewell, late 1930s. This development, on the Earls Hall Estate (in fact on Whitehouse Farm) was part of the large pre-war expansion of the town. In the previous few years Prittlewell, which had been principally farmland – between the town of Southend and Rochford – was becoming absorbed into the ever increasing conurbation. Far from being the 'mother' of Southend, Prittlewell was now being swallowed up in the urban sprawl. (*Reproduced by kind permission of Southend Borough Engineers Department*)

Today, this whole area forms the northern end of Southend, spreading from here westwards along the arterial road towards London. There is now no sign of the farmland which once occupied this area. However, Rochford Road, which can be seen forming the junction with Oaken Grange Drive, follows exactly a very ancient roadway to Rochford, Eastwood and beyond. (*Author*)

Victoria Avenue, at the junction with Fairfax Drive, *c.* 1960. On the right is the Bungalow Restaurant. Tea rooms were first established here in 1923, when Mrs Curtis had the property. She lived in Bridge House, which was situated just to the rear, and it is likely that she established the tea rooms here following the death of her husband. The Bungalow Tea Rooms are first mentioned in 1926. (*Reproduced by kind permission of Southend Borough Engineers Department*)

Although the name changed, a restaurant remained here until 1966. In 1967–8 the premises were taken by A & K Stationery, who still occupy them. It is interesting to note that when the tea rooms were first built, this stretch of the Avenue was still called North Street. It was not changed to Victoria Avenue until 1936–7. (*Author*)

Victoria Avenue, looking north from one of the new office blocks, 1968. At this date the Avenue was still a single carriageway, with large elegant houses lining both sides, and with St Mary's Church, Prittlewell, standing prominently in the background. (*Reproduced by kind permission of Southend Borough Engineers Department*)

In December 1962 plans for the widening of Victoria Avenue into a dual carriageway were discussed, which included plans for an underpass at the junction of East and West Roads. The scheme was planned to begin in 1968–9, with properties on the east side of the Avenue being acquired from 1964. On the right, the old sandpit was converted to the very pleasant Churchill Gardens. Although taken in 1970, this view has changed very little in the intervening years. (*Reproduced by kind permission of Southend Borough Engineers Department*)

A view from the new Civic Centre building, looking south down Victoria Avenue, mid-1960s. In the background can be seen the Keddies 'skyscraper', nearing completion, and to the right the governmental office blocks, also nearing completion. In the foreground on the left is the public library. The Municipal College can be clearly seen in the centre of the photograph. (*Reproduced by kind permission of Southend Museums*)

This view of 1973 shows the new public library and associated car park almost totally obscuring the old public library, which was at this time being converted to the town's Central Museum. On the left in the distance the new multi-storey car park is also complete. (*Reproduced by kind permission of Southend Borough Engineers Department*)

Victoria Avenue, looking north from Victoria Circus, early 1960s. On the right are the small shops of the Victoria Arcade (part of which was called the Talza Arcade), and in the distance can be seen Southend Library. Between the two is Southend Victoria railway station. (*Reproduced by kind permission of Southend Borough Engineers Department*)

Today the view has changed almost completely. The arcade has been replaced by what is now called Victoria Plaza shopping centre, but which was originally the Hammerson development. The only common feature in the two views is the old library building, which today is the Central Museum and Planetarium. (*Author*)

Southend Public Library was opened in 1906, as the town's first free public library. On the first floor was a small museum collection, which today forms the core collection of Southend Museum. The building was designed by H.T. Hare, and financed by the Carnegie Trust. This photograph, taken in about 1920 by Alfred Padgett of Leigh, shows the gardens of the library extending in front of the building to the pavement. The road at this time was a single carriageway. (*Reproduced by kind permission of Southend Museums*)

Today the old library building has been converted to the town's principal museum, the Central Museum and Planetarium. It was opened as such in 1981, and the new central library opened in 1974 on an adjacent site immediately to the north. (*Author*)

CHAPTER TWO

VICTORIA CIRCUS AND HIGH STREET

Victoria Circus was the roundabout at the southern end of the newly constructed Victoria Avenue; to the south was High Street, and to the east Southchurch Road (leading to Shoebury) and to the west, London Road (now the 'old' A13 road). The Circus, on the site of the old Whitegate crossroads, soon acquired the name 'cobweb corner' because of the tram wires and lines, since here was also the central tram office.

High Street began as a private road, serving the newly erected Grand Terrace and Hotel, and linking this new development of the late eighteenth century with the White Gate, at the junction with the main London Road. The building of High Street was part of the arrangement made between the developers of the 'New Town' and the Lord of the Manor. In High Street two public houses were built at this time, the Duchess of York (hence York Road, originally called York Street) and the Duke of Clarence (hence Clarence Street).

High Street was, until the later nineteenth century, a residential road. The principal shops in Southend were still in the Lower Town, along Marine Parade. When Clifftown was built in the later 1850s and early 1860s, shops were built in Nelson Street but still not in High Street. In fact the first main shops in High Street were not constructed until the late 1860s or early 1870s. In 1873, for example, there are advertisements for Godward's nursery shop in High Street and in 1874 Thomas Dowset laid plans before the Southend Local Board for the building of a terrace of shops towards the southern end of High Street. In about 1870 Henry Luker had moved his brewery from 'Brewery Road' to High Street, to a site adjacent to Southend Station. In fact it appears that the earliest shops were built at the southern end of High Street, and then gradually more and more shops spread northwards.

Not until the 1890s was the whole of High Street developed for shopping. By the end of the century the Hotel Victoria had been built on the north-east corner of High Street, thus completing the development of the town's principal commercial thoroughfare.

Southend Technical College was opened in 1902. The architect was H.T. Hare, who also designed the public library (opened 1906) and Prittlewell School in Southend. The College replaced the old Southend Institute buildings in Clarence Road which had been erected in 1884. In 1894 the municipal buildings had been erected on the south side of the Institute, and gradually the municipal work of the new Council was such that they began to encroach on the educational establishment. Originally known as the Southend Day Technical Schools (for boys and girls), in 1913 the girls left to take up residence in new schools, and from that time the building was called the Southend High School for Boys. In 1938 the new boys' school was built in Prince Avenue. Once more the Victoria Circus building became the Technical College. (*Reproduced by kind permission of Southend Museums*)

The college building was demolished as part of the rebuilding of the town centre in the 1960s. Originally it was intended that new buildings on this site would link up with the shopping centre to create a large, integrated centre, but in fact nothing was built on the site for many years. It was used as a car park until plans were eventually passed for the building of the new Odeon cinema and associated shops. The new Odeon opened in 1997. (*Author*)

A view of the 'old' Victoria Circus, photographed by Mr W. Wren in about 1960. Here we have before us the public toilets, to the left of which is Garon's Corner, with Talmage Buildings supporting the Garon's Clock, one of the principal landmarks in the centre of town. Behind here was the Victoria and Talza Arcade. To the right is the Hotel Victoria, on the north-east side of High Street. Mr Wren was standing in front of the old Technical College to take this view. (*Reproduced by kind permission of Mr W. Wren*)

Today the whole area has been redeveloped and pedestrianised. This view, probably better than many, demonstrates the results of the ravages of the town planners of the mid-1960s. Most large towns suffered the same plight as Southend, with the historic heart of the place being ripped apart in the name of 'progress'. Unfortunately, that resulted in the destruction of the unique character of the town. (*Author*)

Opposite above: The Gaumont Cinema in Southchurch Road, adjacent to the Hotel Victoria. The Gaumont replaced the Hippodrome Theatre, which had closed in January 1934. (*Reproduced by kind permission of Southend Museums*)

Opposite below: Following the closure of the Gaumont, the site was first occupied by Bermands, children's outfitters, and from 1964–5 by the supermarket Victor Value. The large building adjacent to Victor Value is Hotel Victoria, which was demolished in the late 1960s. (*Reproduced by kind permission of Southend Museums*)

The site has gone through several changes of use, including Halfords the car accessory store, and the latest venture is a furniture store. The underpass was part of the refashioning of the Victoria Circus area, and links the southern end of Victoria Avenue with Southchurch Road. It passes below the new shopping centre and gives access also to buses and shop deliveries. (*Author*)

The Victoria and Talza arcades from the south-east, with Garon's clock to the left of centre. On the right is the Talmage Buildings; this had been owned by C.H.J. Talmage since the building of the arcades in 1926. The arcade is said to have been built by C.H.J. Talmage, work starting on what had been a builder's yard in 1924 and completed in 1927. It was an arcade of very small shops, of a very wide variety: here was Bobbin's bookshop, Laurence Mathews' art shop and Talmage's own pet shop to name just three out of dozens. Although the arcades were not spotlessly clean by modern standards, there was always something of interest to see, and most people have fond memories of them. There was also a cinema, originally called the Civic News Theatre, but later the New Vic. (*Reproduced by kind permission of Mr W. Wren*)

The arcades were demolished in 1966–8 to make way for the Victoria Plaza shopping centre. On three floors, this comprises a series of large retail chains, together with some smaller specialist shops. In the foreground of the photograph is the Deeping subway, giving vehicular access between the new Victoria Circus and Southchurch Road. One of the main, and unfortunate, features of this shopping complex has been the quite rapid turnover of shops, and the large numbers of unoccupied units. Perhaps things will improve. (*Author*)

A view taken by Mr W. Wren, immediately before the demolition of virtually all the buildings seen in this photograph, late 1960s. Originally known as Cobweb Corner, because of all the overhead tram wires, a later name for this area was Garon's Corner. This name was strictly applied to the north-east corner of Victoria Circus, for it was here that the large Garon's clock was visible from a wide area of the town. Although by this date the Garon's empire was past its peak, earlier it could boast a wide variety of retail shops – fishmongers, greengrocers, butchers, ironmongers, and so on, together with a cinema in High Street. (*Reproduced by kind permission of Mr W. Wren*)

Today the scene seems rather less interesting, probably because of the architecture. The Hotel Victoria was replaced by (yet another) bank, and the fascinating Victoria and Talza arcades were replaced by the Hammerson development, now called Victoria Plaza. The change of name has not helped to improve the comfort of shopping here, especially in the winter months! (*Author*)

The High Street, looking from Victoria Circus, *c.* 1960. On the left is the Hotel Victoria which was opened in 1899, and was designed by James Thompson. The hotel contained 100 rooms, each of which had electric lighting, and steam radiators on each floor kept the building warm in winter. On the opposite corner is Dixons, a family department store much loved by its patrons. Victoria Circus was at the junction of High Street and Victoria Avenue, Southchurch Road to the east, and London Road to the west. (*Reproduced by kind permission of Southend Borough Engineers Department*)

The whole area is now a pedestrian precinct; the Hotel Victoria was demolished in the rebuilding scheme. and Dixons was replaced by W.H. Smith. The whole character of the centre of the town changed with the rebuilding of the late 1960s, followed by pedestrianisation. (*Author*)

The northern end of Southend High Street from a postcard view, *c.* 1915. On the left-hand (west) side we have just part of the Garon's Café visible, adjacent to the Masonic Hall, before the long row of shops begins. The tram lines are clearly visible. (*Reproduced by kind permission of Southend Museums*)

A rather different aspect today, with all of High Street now pedestrianised (from the 1960s). The row of shops on the middle left have remained largely unaltered, but Garon's Café building, together with the Garon's Cinema which was to its left, and the Masonic Hall have long gone, being replaced by 1960s shop buildings and office block above. (*Author*)

G. J. Keddie opened his first shop in Southend in 1892–3. In 1934 a new shop front with large columns was erected, in the style of Selfridges of London. Keddies became one of the town's principal family-run businesses, and one of the biggest department stores in the country. In 1960 Keddies opened the town's (and possibly the country's) first supermarket – SupaSave. Keddies rapidly expanded to take over the whole of the site once occupied by the Strand Cinema and Arcade. In 1987–9 the store was completely refurbished and revamped in order to counter the expected competition from the Royals shopping centre at the other end of High Street. (*Reproduced by kind permission of Southend Museums*)

Keddies closed in 1996. The shop front has been rebuilt to copy the Selfridges style, and part of the ground floor High Street frontage has been taken by Tesco. We still wait to see who will occupy the rest of this very large site. (*Author*)

An early view of the High Street, probably *c.* 1880. On the left can be seen the cottage occupied by Mr George Attridge with his wife Fanny and three children, on the corner of what became Clifftown Road. In the middle distance is the chimney of Luker's Brewery. The firm had moved from the east (Brewery Road, now Southchurch Avenue) to the High Street site in about 1870. The photograph was taken before the extension of the railway to Shoeburyness, and so there is no High Street bridge. At this date only the southernmost end of High Street had been developed for shopping. (*Reproduced by kind permission of Southend Museums*)

This whole corner was redeveloped in the 1960s, when Garon's Tea Bar was swept away and with it all the coal offices. The layout at this junction of Clifftown Road was altered, and large new shop premises now occupy this corner. (*Author*)

Opposite: George Attridge's cottage had been sold for development in the mid-1880s, and Luker's Brewery had been replaced by the Astoria (later Odeon) cinema in the mid-1930s. The railway line, which reached Southend in the mid-1850s, was extended to Shoebury in the 1880s, when the High Street bridge was built. By the end of the nineteenth century the whole length of High Street had been built up and had become the town's principal shopping street. This view, of the late 1950s, shows the same corner from a slightly higher angle. Garon's Tea Bar occupies the corner plot, with the road leading to the railway station being occupied by the offices of the local coal firms. (*Reproduced by kind permission of Southend Borough Engineers Department*)

Another view of Mr Attridge's High Street cottage. The notice on the left side of the building advertises '7 plots of building land' which were developed in the late nineteenth century. It was in the fields behind the cottage that the Essex Agricultural Show had been held in 1881. (*Reproduced by kind permission of Southend Museums*)

A large terrace of shops was built on the site of the cottage and adjoining land. The road to the north, coming off High Street, was originally going to be called Subscription Road but its name was changed to Clifftown Road at the time of its laying, very apt since it leads directly to the northern part of that estate. (*Author*)

Another view of the buildings erected on the site of Attridge's cottage. For many years the premises of outfitters, draper and tailors, between 1938 and 1939 they were taken over by Rossi (not the ice-cream manufacturers) for their milk bar, which remained here until 1968. (*Reproduced by kind permission of Southend Borough Engineers Department*)

Since these premises were vacated by Rossi they have been occupied by various firms, including a draper's again. Recently, as can be seen here, in a reflection of modern trends, the communication firm Orange has secured the shop. (*Author*)

One of the best-known stretches of High Street was that around the premises of R.A. Jones, whose shop was often called 'Jones's Clock' from the clock which can be seen in this photograph, dating from the early years of the twentieth century. Liptons were at 74 High Street from the 1890s. In about 1912/13 the premises had been taken over by the British Shoe Company, and it was in their hands until 1928/9. By 1932 this was Lyons' Tea Shop, which it remained until the 1970s. Beyond Jones's shop was Heddles' Cash Clothing Stores and, beyond that, the London public house. (*Reproduced by kind permission of Southend Museums*)

Both Lyons and Jones changed their shop frontages and the facades above, in order to modernise them and to keep up with fashion, and these have largely remained unchanged. Even now, looking at the very top of the building, you can still see the name 'R.A. Jones'. Another old firm, now long gone, was the tobacconist A. Edwards, and that name also remains at the top of the building a little further down from Jones's. (*Author*)

In 1909 the combined Home and Atlantic Fleets came to Southend, and the whole town celebrated this momentous event. High Street was described as being 'transformed out of all recognition, wreathed in gay colours and adorned with summer flowers'. Even one of the town's tramcars was decorated by Corporation employees to resemble the 'Dreadnought' battleship. (*Reproduced by kind permission of Southend Museums*)

The majority of the buildings which were present in the 1909 view of High Street have been replaced by more modern and much larger structures, reflecting the changes in shopping habits. One of the principal buildings in High Street is the Marks and Spencer building, seen here on the left. It is built on the site of their original 'Penny Bazaar'. (*Author*)

The Golden Boot was, in the late nineteenth century, Southend's premier shoe and boot retailer. This photograph was taken in July 1881. The proprietor was L. Warren, bootmaker, although of course he did not make all the footwear on sale. His neighbours in High Street were T. Belcham, corn chandler, Abraham Godward, seedsman, whose nursery shop was one of the first shops in High Street, John Currie, hairdresser and Charles Woosnam, wine merchant. (*Reproduced by kind permission of Southend Museums*)

By 1906 the Golden Boot had been replaced by the London and South Western Bank, with dentists occupying the upper floor. In 1937 dentists were still occupying the premises and, at no. 38, the Victoria Wine Company were still in residence. British Home Stores opened their first shop on this site in 1938, at 40–4 High Street. Their new and much enlarged premises were opened in 1969, providing 70,000 sq. ft of floor area. (*Author*)

In the late nineteenth century there were many complaints, from those in favour of abstinence, of the rowdy behaviour of drunken men and women in the High Street. The London pub was just one of the public houses frequented. In early February 1941 the London in High Street suffered a direct hit from a German bomb. Much of it was destroyed. In the raid of 19 October 1942 the premises of R.A. Jones, Jeweller, and Heddles' Cash Clothing Stores were also hit. (*Reproduced by kind permission of Echo Newspapers*)

The London public house was renamed the Tavern in the Town in 1969. The premises continued to serve as a public house until 1983. Between that date and 1985 it was almost completely rebuilt, and re-opened in 1985/6 as Clinton Cards. (*Reproduced by kind permission of Echo Newspapers*)

This row of shops was built for Dowsett in the late 1870s, and this corner building was 'Dowsett's General Ironmongery, Pianoforte, China, Glass, Cutlery and House Furnishing Warehouse'. Thomas Dowsett was Southend's first Mayor in 1892. This remained Dowsett's shop (described as 'Stationers' in *Kelly's Directory*) until 1906, when it was taken over by J. Black. (*Reproduced by kind permission of Southend Museums*)

Today this is the Royal Fish Bar, one of the town's principal fish-and-chip shops. The shop is first recorded as a 'Fish Restaurant' in 1972. It is interesting to note that here we have one of the rare survivals of a building from the early days of the town's High Street, virtually intact, even with the original advertising sign in place, although now painted out. (*Author*)

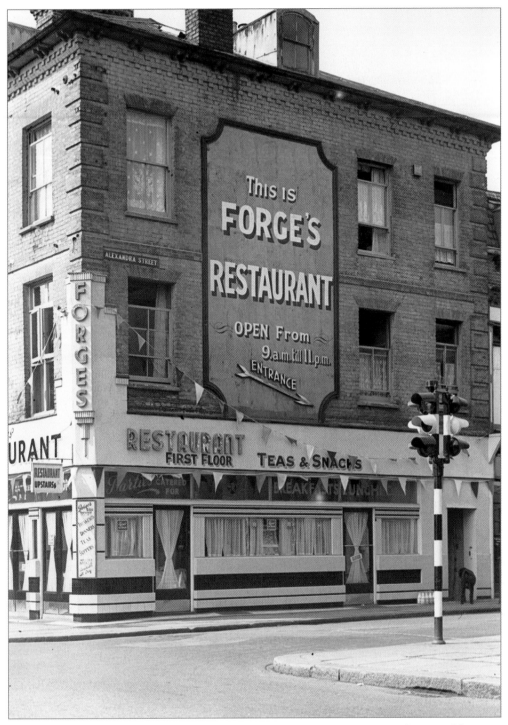

The shop remained a stationers and 'fancy repository' until 1930 or so. In 1939 the ground floor was used as an amusement arcade, the upper floor being a ladies' hairdressers. Some time between 1940 and 1950 it became Forge's Restaurant, owned by Harold Forge, and remained so until about 1970. (*Reproduced by kind permission of Southend Borough Engineers Department*)

Robert Arthur Jones took over an existing jewellery business at 78 High Street in 1890, and in 1903 purchased the shop next door, building the business up to become the 'County Jewellers'. He was very interested in sport, particularly cricket and football. In 1893 he was instrumental in the formation of the Southend and District School's League (and sponsored the Borough sports), and he became known as 'the children's friend'. He was prominent in many of the town's sporting clubs and associations as well as being one of the founders of the Southend Chamber of Commerce. In 1913 he purchased land in the north of the town for a sports ground in memory of his wife; it is known as the Jones Memorial Ground. In 1917 he purchased Prittlewell Priory for the town as a museum. (*Reproduced by kind permission of Southend Museums*)

R.A. Jones died in 1925, his sons taking over the business. The firm finally closed in about 1980. Immediately to the south of Jones's was, in the early part of the century, Lipton's tea shop; later this was taken over by J. Lyons restaurant. In more recent times the site has been occupied by McDonalds. It must be unusual for the one building to have such a continuity of use. (*Author*)

Looking northwards along High Street, towards the junction with Alexandra Street, July 1881. The flags are celebrating the coming to Southend of the Essex Agricultural Show, which was held in a field opposite the railway station! Nearest to the camera is the shop of Joseph Packman, draper, who lived above the shop with his wife. His shop assistants were Ann Woodley and Lucretia Fuller; he also had an apprentice, Henry Guiver and servant, Ruth Pratt. Next door is Thomas Barrett, bank agent; beyond the bank is Young's wine merchants, then William Lodder, watchmaker. At the far end of the block is Thomas Dowsett's shop. (*Reproduced by kind permission of Southend Museums*)

This parade of shop buildings, although now much altered, is the oldest surviving group in High Street. The second shop from the left is now Southend's Tourist Information Centre, occupying Thomas Barrett's bank. Again, notice that on the whole the upper floors have remained largely intact. (*Author*)

At the southern end of Southend High Street, on the eastern side, were some of the town's premier stores, and the first area of High Street to be developed for shopping. Here was Tipper's restaurant, described in 1899 as a 'Southend Mecca for single men – A Haven of Luxury'. Apart from its forty bedrooms ('equipped in the best taste') there was a ballroom, with mirrors fitted all round, which could double up as a restaurant for up to 400 diners. On the first floor was the lounge, decorated in 'Moorish' style, with Axminster carpet and painted ceiling. To the north was Cotgrove's restaurant and tea rooms, while further to the north the sweet shop of George Isaac (manufacturer of the first 'Southend Rock'), and then the photographic studios of Alfred Shepherd. Further on still are the two early bank buildings with queues forming outside! (*Reproduced by kind permission of Southend Museums*)

By the 1970s this whole area had become rather run-down, particularly since the opening of the new shopping centre at the northern end of High Street. The whole of this side of High Street was swept away in the early 1980s for the development of a new shopping centre – the Royals. The name was adopted from the earlier buildings on the site – the Royal Library, Royal Stores and, on the opposite side of the road, the Royal Terrace and Hotel. (*Author*)

The southern end of High Street, photographed by Frank Secourable in about 1875. On the left is the Royal Hotel, and opposite is Prospect House, built in about 1820, the home of Elizabeth Heygate and later Warwick Deeping, the famous author. High Street had originally been laid out as part of the scheme for the New Town of Southend in the early to mid-1790s, but it did not become the town's main shopping street until the late nineteenth century. Until then it was still partly residential. (*Reproduced by kind permission of Southend Museums*)

In the mid-1980s the whole of the southern end of the east side of High Street was demolished to make way for the Royals shopping centre. Prospect House and other, later nineteenth century properties, were swept away in a scheme which also saw the demise of Grove Road, the Ritz cinema and the Grand Pier Hotel. (*Author*)

Southend's first General Post Office building, in Weston Road, was opened in 1896. Tenders had been invited for the building of the General Post Office in May 1895. The new Post Office was built in the grounds of the old lodge, which can still be seen from the alley on the Clifftown Road side. The post office was to have a frontage of 50 ft, the 'public room' being 37 ft by 23 ft wide. 'Here provision has been made suitable for the requirements of Southend probably for many years.' (*From the* Southend Standard, *23 May 1895. Reproduced by kind permission of Southend Libraries*)

This post office closed in the late 1980s, being replaced by a much smaller 'shop' in the Victoria Circus (Hammerson) development. This in turn closed, to be replaced by a new post office and shop in High Street. The post office building in Weston Road was converted into a public house called, very appropriately, The Last Post. (*Reproduced by kind permission of Southend Museums*)

Market Place, looking north towards Alexandra Street, *c.* 1960. Market Place had originally been part of the scheme put forward by the local businessman (today we would call him an entrepreneur) Thomas Dowsett, in 1874, and was the small roadway to the west and south of his series of terraced shops fronting High Street. (*Reproduced by kind permission of Southend Borough Engineers Department*)

After many years of almost total neglect, Market Place has gone through something of a mini-revival in recent years. Several small shops and cafés have opened up, and market stalls are now to be seen near the High Street end. (*Author*)

This photograph of Alexandra Street was taken during the visit to Southend of the Home and Atlantic Fleet in 1909. The principal streets were decorated in suitable fashion. We are looking eastwards towards High Street. Alexandra Street was then relatively new, having been laid out in 1873, and together with High Street was one of the principal shopping streets in the town. In 1909 you could find here the Singer Sewing Machine Co., Schofield and Martins, the Empire Theatre and the Victoria Temperance and Commercial Hotel. (*Reproduced by kind permission of Southend Museums*)

Architecturally the road has changed very little. Although there are still some specialist shops here, it is by no means as busy now as in the past. However, it is certainly worth a visit for its architecture alone. (*Author*)

Southend's first police station was built in 1873 in Alexandra Street, just off High Street. Here we see the front of the station being prepared for protection with sandbags against air raids during the Second World War. (*Reproduced by kind permission of Echo Newspapers*)

Along with several other buildings in this stretch, this police station was demolished following the opening of the new police headquarters in Victoria Avenue in 1962. The site of the old police station is now partly a road (from Royal Mews) and partly a car park. Some of the buildings beyond remain council offices, part of the early complex of such offices reflecting the growth of council work during the twentieth century. (*Author*)

The Royal Hotel in High Street, with a coach and four standing at the entrance. The coach was driven by Percy (Stan) Gill; his father apparently ran the first horse-drawn bus service in Southend in the nineteenth century. Rather earlier, at the end of the eighteenth century, two coach companies vied for trade in the newly expanding settlement, the journey from London taking about eight hours. (*Reproduced by kind permission of Southend Museums*)

The hotel was extensively restored in the 1970s. The second entrance to the hotel, seen on the right in the top photograph, has now been moved even further to the right, into what is now named Caroline House, after Princess Caroline, who stayed here in the early years of the nineteenth century. The hotel is now empty and its future at present is uncertain. (*Author*)

A photograph by Frank Henry Secourable of about 1875, showing the Royal Library, with the corner of Grove Terrace just visible behind, and in the distance, St John's Church. The Library and Grove Terrace were part of the scheme for 'New Southend' and were built in the late eighteenth century, together with the Grand Terrace and Hotel, and High Street. St John's was built as the parish church of Southend, being opened in 1842 when Southend was created a parish in its own right. (*Reproduced by kind permission of Southend Museums*)

Grove Terrace had been demolished in the later nineteenth century, and the old library building had been greatly altered by the mid-twentieth century. In the early 1980s it was decided to revive the southern end of High Street by demolishing all the buildings on the eastern side to create space for the building of the Royals shopping centre. St John's Church is now hidden away, and largely forgotten, between the Royals and the Palace Hotel. (*Author*)

CHAPTER THREE

TO THE WEST

Following the arrival of the railway at Southend in 1856, the land immediately to the south of Southend station was leased by the railway company (Peto, Brassey and Betts) for the building of Southend's first housing estate – Clifftown. Thus began the development of Westcliff. The building of the railway line and this estate, and those that quickly followed, had two immediate effects. The first was the creation of a core of commuters, who could now live at the seaside and travel to London to look after their businesses. The second result, a little longer in arriving, was the huge increase in holiday traffic. Particularly following the Bank Holiday Act of 1871, the numbers of trippers to Southend from the east end of London rose enormously. On Bank Holiday weekends (particularly August Bank Holiday) the numbers of visitors far outstripped the residents.

The Park Estate was the second main housing scheme in Westcliff; this was built around the Southend Park, the outlines of which can still be traced, and is reflected by the names of the roads on each side. One side, Avenue Road, was in fact the old 'chaseway' leading down to the windmill of the Lord of the Manor of Milton Hall (Nazareth House now occupies the site of the manor house).

The local authority was determined to exclude what they termed the 'lower class of excursionists' from the western part of the borough, and particularly to retain the newly built Western Esplanade for the healthy constitutional and the 'better class' of visitor. Thus it was that the pier marked the division between the eastern and western parts of the seafront.

Our photographic journey starts west of High Street, to Hamlet Court Road, and then down to the seafront and towards the pier.

Royal Terrace and Hotel was built in the early 1790s, as part of the scheme promoted by the Lord of the Manor of Milton and Prittlewell (Daniel Scratton) for the creation of a 'New Southend'. It was hoped to attract more genteel visitors to the growing town by providing accommodation more in keeping with their refined tastes. However, the venture was not an immediate success, and the whole estate was sold in lots in 1800. The principal purchasers were the Heygate family. In the opening years of the nineteenth century the Terrace was visited by Princess Caroline (wife of the Prince Regent), after which the terrace and hotel became 'Royal', and by Lady Hamilton (of Lord Nelson fame). (*Reproduced by kind permission of Southend Museums*)

During the Second World War the terrace was taken over by the admiralty, as HMS *Leigh*, from which control of convoys took place. In later years the buildings became rather neglected and there was talk of them being demolished. A campaign was launched in the town to preserve the buildings, leading to the formation of the Southend Society and the creation of Southend's conservation area, of which this is part. (*Author*)

Bomb damage in the Second World War to buildings in Clarence Road, just north of the old Southend Council buildings. Originally this site had been laid out as the Alexandra Skating Rink in 1873, next to the Victoria Coffee Palace. Later the Southend Institute (successor of the Mechanics' Institute) was built here, and later the first council offices – following the creation of the Borough of Southend in 1892. (*Reproduced by kind permission of Echo Newspapers*)

Since the demolition of the old council offices, the site has been a car park. The council moved its operations into the new Civic Centre building in Victoria Avenue, which was opened by HRH the Queen Mother in 1967. (*Author*)

Clifftown, with Clifftown Congregational Church on the eastern side, is seen here from the west in about 1900, with the flower and vegetable gardens of the residents in the middle. It was these gardens that the Southend donkeys would make for when they escaped from their tethers. The area was laid out as Southend's first housing estate following the arrival of the railway in 1856. Here the first commuters lived in the later nineteenth century. (*Reproduced by kind permission of Southend Museums*)

Clifftown has changed little; it was the town's first, and principal, conservation zone. It is impossible to get precisely the same view as the earlier one, because of the trees and, behind the trees, a café and clubhouse for the bowling green, which now occupies the site of the gardens. (*Author*)

Nelson Street, photographed by Frank Henry Secourable in about 1875. Before the development of High Street for shopping, Nelson Street was the principal shopping street in what was known as 'Upper' Southend (to distinguish it from the Lower town, along Marine Parade). This area, Clifftown, was built between 1856 and 1861. It was designed by the firm of Banks and Barry and built by Lucas Brothers. Among the shops in this street were Fred Garon, plumber, George Gooch, grocer, John Fleming, poulterer, Charles Taylor, stationer and William Griffin, grocer. (*Reproduced by kind permission of Southend Museums*)

Today only one shop front exists intact, that being the shop nearest the railway line. Although the layout of the street has remained unaltered, the majority of the premises have now been taken over by solicitors firms and, from being the most bustling part of the town, it has become a very quiet back street. (*Author*)

At the corner of North Road and London Road, in 1924, we see the premises of J. Leeson. He opened his book, wardrobe and furniture shop at 215 North Road in 1907/8. In 1911 the address is recorded as 27 North Road, and by 1914 1 Leigh Road East. The reason for the changes in address is not that he kept moving premises, but that the road numbering system changed as the area was developed. In 1920 the address was 207 London Road, when he is simply described as a furniture dealer. In the 1930s he moved his shop to the Talza Arcade, where he opened as a bookseller. (*Photograph reproduced by kind permission of Essex Record Office, D/BC 1.4.10/26/181*)

Over the years the shops have been extended forward, making the pavement quite narrow on the London Road side. At the beginning of the twenty-first century many of these shop units are empty, giving a rather neglected and depressing aspect to the corner. It is interesting to note that in the Middle Ages this was a major crossroads linking Prittlewell, Milton, Chalkwell and Leigh. (*Author*)

Although we do not know the exact date of this photograph, it was taken in about 1920 at the corner of Milton Street and London Road in Westcliff, when there appears to have been a flood. Crowds are watching a man paddling across the road. This small parade of shops, up to the junction with Milton Street, was known in the early twentieth century as Cheapside, the corner being Cheapside Corner, which was the premises of the Perhams for the first half of the century. The complex array of tram wires at this junction is quite evident. (*Reproduced by kind permission of Southend Museums*)

The corner group of shops was completely rebuilt in the 1970s; the whole of this area has in fact seen a considerable amount of remodelling, much of it relating to the increase in traffic. (*Author*)

This view of the corner of Kings Road and Crowstone Road, looking towards Genesta Road, in Westcliff, was photographed by Southend Borough Engineer's Department in 1906. We can see a number of houses being constructed, the builder of the corner plot being R. Elvy and Son, of Christchurch Road. Most of the houses in Genesta Road were designed by A.C. Cooke. (*Photograph reproduced by kind permission of Essex Record Office, D/BC 1/4/10/20/86*)

The same view today. The principal difference, apart from the growth of the trees, is the traffic. It is doubtful whether the architects and civil engineers of the earlier period could have envisaged the enormous growth in traffic which we have witnessed in the twentieth century. (*Author*)

Hamlet Court Road, decorated for the visit of the Home and Atlantic Fleets, 1909. This road was often referred to as Southend's second High Street, with a number of specialist, elegant and high class shops, including, for example, the millinery establishment of Pedrette and Williams. (*Reproduced by kind permission of Southend Museums*)

From the 1980s some of the old established shops began to close down, while others have managed to remain in business. Probably because of changes in shopping habits, and the availability of out-of-town supermarkets and shopping centres, such once-flourishing shopping streets are changing. (*Author*)

A postcard view showing 'The Gardens, New Parade, Westcliff-on-Sea', *c*. 1915. In 1902 tenders had been invited for the construction of the sea wall and Esplanade in front of the Chalkwell Hall Estate and for the extension of the Western Esplanade. The scheme included the laying out of enclosed gardens. (*Reproduced by kind permission of Southend Museums*)

The view has changed very little in the intervening years. The principal differences that can be seen are the housing developments on the right-hand side, the construction of shops on the beach side, and the absence of the iron hand-rail on the sea wall, which has been completely rebuilt. (*Author*)

The Esplanade at Westcliff-on-Sea, probably *c.* 1910. Here we see those people called by the local authorities the 'better class of excursionists' taking their stroll in the fresh air. Although there are a few people on the beach, sunbathing was still a long way into the future; most are promenading, and, of course, all wearing hats. (*Reproduced by kind permission of Southend Museums*)

Fewer people today take to promenading along the seafront, even on the nicest of days. The car now makes it so easy to travel considerable distances for a day out, and there are so many other leisure activities available for all the family. (*Author*)

The Esplanade and Overcliff Hotel, Westcliff-on-Sea, *c.* 1925. The Overcliff Hotel had been opened in 1923. In the *Homeland Guide* to Southend-on-Sea, of the mid-1950s, the Overcliff is described as being equipped with private rooms and ballroom, which was available for banquets and wedding receptions. In 1931 the *Official Guide* to Southend published advertisements for a total of thirty-three hotels (including the Overcliff) and nearly 130 boarding houses in the town. (*Reproduced by kind permission of Southend Museums*)

During the 1960s and afterwards the holiday trade in Southend declined quite rapidly. The Overcliff Hotel was demolished in the early 1970s to make way for the flats shown here. (*Author*)

An interesting view of Western Esplanade, *c.* 1902, before the widening schemes were carried out. The sea wall was built in 1905. In the distance can be seen the Palmeira Towers Hotel, which was demolished in 1978. (*Reproduced by kind permission of Southend Museums*)

Today, although the view has changed somewhat, with the widening of the roadway, and the block of flats replacing the hotel, it is interesting to note that the original rails remain along the top of this stretch of sea wall. (*Author*)

The widening of Western Esplanade included the construction of this seating platform in 1911. This photograph was taken for Southend's Borough Engineer's Department as a record of the work on the Esplanade. The Council had applied to the Local Government Board for a loan of £50,000 for the work. (*Photograph reproduced by kind permission of Essex Record Office, D/BC 1/4/10/7/17*)

The platform is well patronised throughout the summer months, with a first aid post occupying a prominent position. The beach and foreshore are certainly more attractive today, as can be seen here, with large quantities of imported sand to make sunbathing a more comfortable experience! (*Author*)

THE BANDSTAND, SOUTHEND-ON-SEA.

Opposite above: The bandstand at Westcliff. The original bandstand here was erected in 1902 and was built by F. and E. Davey at a cost of £425. (*Reproduced by kind permission of Southend Museums*)

Opposite below: The second, larger bandstand was built by Walter Macfarlane & Co. of Glasgow, costing £750, and was opened in 1909. Known as the 'wedding cake' bandstand, it was a favourite meeting place. A season ticket would have cost you 6s, while a daily admission cost 2d (3d on a weekend evening). The 1902 bandstand was removed to the foot of the cliffs, in the area known as Happy Valley. By this date Southend could boast a total of about six bandstands: on Pawley's Green, two on the pier, one in the Kursaal (although this may have been removed by this date), the Westcliff bandstand and the Happy Valley bandstand. (*Reproduced by kind permission of Southend Museums*)

The Westcliff bandstand was demolished in 1956. In 1990 the new bandstand was opened on the site of the 1909 version, and today many people enjoy the summer concerts, band competitions and other musical events. The covered area surrounding the bandstand is also used for extra seating and for occasional functions. (*Author*)

Happy Valley, Southend-on-Sea

Opposite above: This view shows Happy Valley, Southend. During the Edwardian period in particular, crowds would gather to watch pierrots, minstrels and other groups of entertainers which so well summed up seaside entertainment. Southend was no exception, with a number of bandstands along various parts of the seafront and on the pier. Here we see the earliest bandstand on this site. This was just below the site of the modern bandstand, on the cliffs. (*Reproduced by kind permission of Southend Museums*)

Opposite below: In 1909 a new bandstand was opened on the cliffs, and the old bandstand was moved down to the Happy Valley, replacing the earlier one there. This became the home of Chirgwin, the 'White-eyed Kaffir'. To see the entertainment you could either pay and have a seat, or, as many people preferred, stand in the area behind and watch from there for nothing. (*Reproduced by kind permission of Southend Museums*)

Happy Valley was later replaced by the Floral Hall at the base of the cliffs. This was destroyed by fire in the 1930s. Today the Happy Valley site is long forgotten, and largely masked by trees. (*Author*)

The Alexandra Yacht Club had been formed in 1873 by a group of well-known Southend dignitaries and held meetings in premises in Alexandra Street, Southend. It was originally called the Alexandra Club, and had two rooms – one for billiards and the other for reading. The founders of the club included Sir Frederick Carne Rasch, MP, Sir William Lloyd Wise, E.A. Wedd and Sir Frederick Heygate. Most of these, and the other founder members, were sufficiently wealthy to be yacht owners, and consequently a large amount of unofficial racing took place; by 1878 the emphasis on yachting led to the change in name of the club, and the new Clubhouse on the cliffs was opened on Trafalgar Day, 21 October 1884. (*Reproduced by kind permission of Southend Museums*)

The Clubhouse still survives on the cliffs and, although modernised, has retained the original structure built by Baker and Wiseman of Southend at a cost of just under £1,000. (*Author*)

CHAPTER FOUR

THE PIER

Following several years of argument, the foundation stone of Southend's first pier was laid in 1829. This pier, built entirely of wood, was just 500 yds long. Further out, in deeper water, was originally moored a boat, called *The Clarence*, later replaced by a wooden structure, The Mount. This acted as a landing stage, passengers being rowed to the pier head. The pier was used not only for passengers, but also for goods, and a tollhouse had been built at the pier entrance. The original Pier Acts provide a lengthy list of the goods and the tariffs that would have to be paid for transporting goods: among the more unusual goods might be numbered a harpsichord, tariff *2s 6d*, a grindstone, *4s ½d*, a turtle, *5s*, and a hundredweight of treacle, *2s ½d*.

In the 1880s the Southend Local Board took the brave decision to have a new pier built. The old wooden structure, which had been lengthened to 1¼ miles in 1846, was feeling the strain, particularly after several years of a horse-drawn tram. Sir James Brunlees was appointed engineer, and in 1889 a new iron and steel pier was completed. There was much discussion about the mode of transport which should be used for the pier. Many years before one of the Board members, Mr Morris, had suggested the use of electricity for powering the trams, a suggestion which at the time appears to have been treated with some derision and disbelief, especially after Mr Morris claimed that this substance could also be used for lighting the town!

Eventually the new pier was fully opened to the public in August 1890, together with an electric tram (the first of its kind on any pier in the world) and pavilion. In the closing years of the nineteenth century the pier was extended into deeper water, as more and larger passenger steamers called. An upper deck was built on the extension in 1908, and a further, eastern, extension built in 1929.

The iron and steel pier has suffered many disasters in its long history, the worst being the two fires which destroyed first, in 1959, the pavilion and second, in 1976, the pier head superstructure. Some of the photographs in this section will show the results of those tragedies.

Opposite above: In the nineteenth century the beach just to the west of the pier was used throughout the winter for storing bathing machines and boats. In the summer the bathing machines were hired out to customers by their proprietors, who paid a licence fee to the Council for their 'pitch' on the beach. In the background, at the foot of the 'shrubbery', below Royal Terrace, can be seen Ingram's hot water baths. At this date there was a single narrow road to the west of the pier. Despite this, the area was always recognised as the 'nicer' part of the seafront, and was patronised by what the late Victorian authorities termed the 'better class of excursionists'. (*Reproduced by kind permission of Southend Museums*)

Opposite below: The same scene in summer, with the boats and bathing machines in full use. Notice particularly the mechanical winch in the foreground of this photograph, used for pulling up bathing machines and movable jetties which gave access to the many pleasure boats. This view (of the 1880s) also shows typical costume of the period, long before the fashion of sunbathing and 'beach wear'. (*Reproduced by kind permission of Southend Libraries*)

The Western Esplanade was first laid out in the 1880s. However, it was not until the opening years of the twentieth century that the widening schemes were adopted. The first part to be widened was at the Chalkwell (western) end, the stretch from Palmeira Parade to the Pier being widened from 1910 onwards. (*Author*)

A view of the beach immediately to the west of the pier by George Dawson, 1900. On the left in the background can be seen the scaffolding around the rising Hotel Metropole. It is interesting to note that, at this time, people did not wear special beach clothes. They sat on the beach, among the boats, or on chairs, in their outdoor day clothes and, of course, all wearing hats. The beach was used as much for storage of boats and bathing machines as for people's recreation, especially in the area immediately adjacent to the pier. (*Reproduced by kind permission of Southend Museums*)

The same view taken today illustrates the great contrast in our beach attire and habits. It seems to have been in the 1930s that we began the practice of sunbathing, exposing more and more of our bodies to the sun. In the background can be seen the rides of Peter Pan's Playground, which occupies the site of the Sunken Gardens. (*Author*)

EDWAY AND SUNKEN GARDENS FROM THE PIER.

The Sunken Gardens, on the west side of the pier, were originally constructed in 1918. The gardens were converted to a children's playground, which was opened by the Mayor, Alderman W. Miles, in July 1924. In his speech the Mayor said that 'the great assistance they rendered to parents and the delight they gave to the children had been abundantly demonstrated'. Later the playground became Peter Pan's Playground, with a variety of amusements, including a speedway track and a small zoo. (*Reproduced by kind permission of Southend Museums*)

Today Peter Pan's Playground offers the visitor a wide range of rides and the most modern scream-inducing experiences. But, as can be seen in this photograph, the racing track is a very firm favourite. (*Author*)

Southend Pier, *c.* 1895. The new iron and steel structure, designed by James Brunlees, had been completed in 1890. The only part of the old wooden pier to survive had been the magnificent brick entrance of 1885. The seafront road at this time extended only as far as the pier, from the east; immediately to the west of the pier, as can be seen on this photograph, shops and stalls occupied the grassy banks and beach. These included the beach studio of Ephraim Lawton, one of Southend's earliest professional photographers; his studio is the middle building of the three shown here. In 1893 the Council recommended that that the number of licences for stalls and standings on the beach be reduced, and that Mr Lawton should satisfactorily repair his studio and 'confine his business entirely to photography'. (*Reproduced by kind permission of Southend Museums*)

Today the seafront road has cut through the old sand banks and grassy slopes; the brick entrance to the Pier was demolished in 1930–1, and the sea immediately to the west of the pier was reclaimed to create what is now Peter Pan's Playground. The pier pavilion was destroyed by fire in 1959; it had been replaced by a ten-pin bowling alley, but that, too, was burnt down recently, and nothing yet has been erected in its place. (*Author*)

A view of the beach immediately to the west of the old wooden pier, *c.* 1880. This pier had originally been constructed in 1829–30, and in this view you can see the original entrance, little more than a shed. On the beach are a range of shops and stalls, including Ephraim Lawton's photographic studios and Ingram's warm baths to the left, in front of which are a number of bathing machines. (*Reproduced by kind permission of Southend Museums*)

The new pier was built alongside the wooden structure, which was then removed. The area of beach to the west was later reclaimed and converted into a sunken garden and children's playground. When the boating pool was constructed on the east side of the pier, a road was built around the southern perimeter. A large workshop building now obscures much of the view towards the shore. (*Author*)

Opposite above: The original wooden pier, constructed in 1829–30, was just 500 yards long, with a shingle 'hard' linking the end of the pier with the separate head or 'mont' built in deep water. In 1846, the pier structure was extended to a mile and a quarter, as shown in this photograph of about 1880. On the east side was the pier harbour, and at this time the entrance was little more than a wooden shed. (*Reproduced by kind permission of Southend Museums*)

Opposite below: Southend was always the most popular destination of visitors from London, particularly the East End. On special events, like this Regatta Day of 12 September 1900, the pier heaved under the burden of people. This was, in fact, the thirty-fourth annual regatta and 'from early evening visitors flocked into the town; railways and steamboats furnishing large quotas, the Lower Town soon presented a bank holiday appearance'. There were sailing events, rowing races and swimming contests, as well as other sports, which took place in the marine Park. (*Reproduced by kind permission of Southend Museums*)

The long and checkered history of Southend's famous pier is now told in the Southend Pier Museum, which is housed in the old pier workshops below the north (shore) station concourse. The pier remains Southend's most famous landmark, a tribute to its Victorian engineers and builders, and is now protected as a Grade II listed building by English Heritage. (*Author*)

The upper level of Pier Hill with the Grand Pier Hotel on the right, Westcliff Motor Services to its left, and the Royal Stores (public house) and seafood stall on the corner. Just to the right of centre is the statue of Queen Victoria, which was the central feature of this area from 1898. In that year the statue was unveiled, to commemorate the Diamond Jubilee of the Queen. The statue was paid for by the Mayor of the time, Bernard Wiltshire Tollhurst. The Queen is seen pointing out into the Estuary, and to her Empire. (*Reproduced by kind permission of Southend Borough Engineers Department*)

The statue was removed in later years, to a site along the cliffs towards Westcliff. Apparently it was said that, far from pointing to the Empire, the Queen was pointing to the public toilets, the steps to which can be seen in the foreground. Some people would say that was quite convenient! All of this area was redeveloped in the early 1980s, the site now being occupied by The Royals shopping complex. (*Author*)

The Pier Hill Fairground from the pier, *c.* 1890. Here we see the 'switchback railway', which was among the varied attractions in this fairground, including 'swings, roundabouts, aerial railways, shooting galleries, cocoa-nut shies, booths, caravans', which are mentioned in a description of the fairground published in 1908, many years after its removal. The fair, and particularly the large switchback railway ride, caused considerable concern for at least one resident who wrote in a letter to the *Southend Standard* about the 'hideous looking contrivance', giving the town 'a cheap, paltry, "all the fun of the fair" appearance to the place'. Just right of middle there is a 'penny' photographic machine. (*From the Noakes Collection; reproduced by kind permission of John Kennedy Melling*)

In 1891 a Mr Bell was appointed as architect for a new hotel to be built on the site of the fairground. He was soon replaced as architect by Mr Chancellor, of Chelmsford, and a design by James Thornton was accepted. There was some difficulty in removing the fairground, but eventually the hotel was begun, under the name of Hotel Metropole. When completed, the hotel was taken over by the Tollhursts, and renamed the Palace Hotel. (*Author*)

H.M. Queen Mary's Naval Hospital, Southend-on-Sea

Opposite above: The Hotel Metropole was begun in the closing years of the nineteenth century, being built for Mr Chancellor of Chelmsford, and designed by James Thornton. Opening at Whitsun 1904, the hotel had cost nearly £300,000. But this had been too much for Mr Chancellor and the scheme was rescued by Alfred Tollhurst, who purchased the building to open it as the Palace Hotel. (*Reproduced by kind permission of Southend Museums*)

Opposite below: At the outbreak of the First World War Alfred Tollhurst offered the Palace Hotel to the military authorities, for use as a hospital. Thus, during the period of hostilities, the hotel was converted to the Queen Mary Royal Naval Hospital. (*Reproduced by kind permission of Southend Museums*)

Although still functioning as a hotel, there are now plans to refurbish the building to something approaching its former splendour. It is a magnificent building and is a landmark from many areas of Southend and, of course, from the sea. (*Author*)

THE PIER HEAD, SOUTHEND ON SEA.

Opposite above: The pier head should really be described as the 'new' pier head, for it was built on the extension to the 1889 structure. The extension was constructed in 1897–8, into deeper water to enable more and larger vessels to call at Southend 'at all states of the tide' and making the pier 1⅓ miles in length. The cost was just over £17,000. In 1908 an upper deck was built on the new pier head, complete with bandstand: 'no seaside town in this country possesses anything of so elaborate and unique a character'. (*Reproduced by kind permission of Southend Museums*)

Opposite below: In 1929 another, eastern, extension was built, known as the Prince George extension. Over the next forty years or so more and more structures were added to the pier head, including restaurants and theatres, and an upper deck to the Prince George extension was a favourite sunbathing place, being called the sun deck. (*Reproduced by kind permission of Southend Museums*)

The pier emerged virtually unscathed from the Second World War, but in 1976 a disastrous fire destroyed all of the superstructure on the pier head. At the time of writing there are still no permanent structures in place. (*Author*)

Opposite above: In 1902 a waterchute had been built on the east side of the pier by Mr Mann. It must be assumed that it was never a very popular attraction, for it was taken down in 1905. (*Reproduced by kind permission of Southend Museums*)

Opposite below: Following the removal of the waterchute, the basin was converted to a boating pool, as seen in this photograph by Alfred Padgett, of about 1920. To the left can be seen the camera obscura, which had been given a licence in the late nineteenth century. Here you could go inside and see the people milling about the seafront, their images projected on to the interior walls by a form of periscope mounted in the centre. (*Reproduced by kind permission of Southend Museums*)

A replica of the *Golden Hind* was built in the old water chute basin in 1949, and it was used for displaying Madame Tussaud's wax effigies of the famous, and historic tableaux. More recently the *Golden Hind* has been replaced by another replica, the *Queen Anne's Revenge*. (*Author*)

The old waterchute basin on the side of the pier had been used as a boating pool ever since the waterchute was taken down in the early years of the twentieth century. In 1949 a full-sized replica of Francis Drake's *Golden Hind* was built for J. & T. Maxwell Ltd, who had been tenants of the boating pool since about 1920. It was built by twelve local seamen, following the idea put forward by William South. Wax figures of Francis Drake and his crew were made by the Tussaud family. (*Reproduced by kind permission of Southend Museums*)

The *Queen Anne's Revenge*, which has now replaced the *Golden Hind*, was the flagship of the notorious pirate known as Blackbeard. Born in Bristol in the 1680s, his real name was Edward Teach. He left England to try his luck as a privateer in the waters around Jamaica. Following a blockade of Charleston, Blackbeard sunk his ship – the *Queen Anne's Revenge* – in 1718. The remains of his ship have recently been discovered in an inlet at Beafort, North Carolina. (*Author*)

The pier illuminations, from the upper deck on the pier head. The pier was one of the main attractions during Southend's first illuminations scheme of the mid-1930s, featuring, for example, Neptune in his undersea world. Ever since then the pier, particularly the pier head, was a draw for thousands of visitors each summer, coming by train and boat, principally from London. With a huge variety of attractions at the pier head, including restaurants, theatres, a museum and amusements, together with the sun deck, the pier was one of the principal destinations for the tourist. (*Reproduced by kind permission of Southend Museums*)

With the decline in visitors throughout the 1960s, the number of ships calling at the pier diminished, the last regular boat trips recorded being in 1969, when just over 4,500 passengers were brought to the pier by boat. When the fire of 1976 destroyed all the buildings on the pier head, they were not rebuilt. (*Author*)

The Children's Boating Lake, east of the pier, was constructed in 1929–30, in time for the 1930 summer season. This was part of the project to build a sea wall and roadway under the pier and to enclose the sunken gardens on the west side of the pier. The boating pool was leased to J. & T. Maxwell initially for a five year period. The new facility first appeared in Southend's official guidebook in 1931. (*Reproduced by kind permission of Southend Museums*)

Following a decline in visitor numbers in the 1970s, the boating lake became disused and rather an eyesore for several years. Eventually it was drained and converted as an extension of Peter Pan's Playground to become Adventure Island in 1998. (*Author*)

The heyday of the boating lake was probably in the 1950s, the approximate date of this photograph. Who can forget the voice of the man operating the loudhailer: 'Come in number three, your time is up'? In those days the seafront heaved with enormous numbers of visitors, and the summers always appeared to be hotter, drier and longer than today's! (*Reproduced by kind permission of Southend Museums*)

As visitor numbers began to fall, with the growth of cheap package holidays abroad, the boating lake became redundant. Today, however, the area now resounds to different cries, mainly young people screaming as they get hurtled along or up and down on ingeniously frightening rides at Adventure Island. (*Author*)

CHAPTER FIVE

TO THE EAST

Marine Parade is the oldest of Southend's esplanades, having been constructed in 1878. Before this date, of course, the road was an important thoroughfare, being the site, before the arrival of the railway and building of Clifftown, of the principal shops, public houses and accommodation in Southend. Some of the early nineteenth-century houses (now much altered) and public houses survive.

In 1902 the Borough Engineer laid before the Council a scheme for 'the widening of the Marine Parade, and the construction of an outer sea wall to effect a considerable reclamation of the Foreshore. . . . The present provision for the reception of the usual summer daily crowds consists merely of the Marine Parade, a narrow road of about 37 feet wide, and a gravelled enclosure or esplanade. Congestion is common, discomfort must be experienced, and the absence of spacious surroundings, where ease and comfort can be obtained, must reduce the general enjoyment . . .'

In order to improve matters it was proposed to increase the width of the road and to enclose a section of the foreshore, creating a 'Pleasure Ground'. The first part of the scheme was to deal with that area from opposite the gas works (Darlow's Green) right along the front to include the first part of Western Esplanade, virtually doubling the existing width of the roadway. The scheme would also include a 'Marine Lake' and have space for gardens, shrubberies, bandstands and other entertainments.

Finally, the scheme would involve the laying out of some of the 'Greens', which had been purchased from their private owners at the end of the nineteenth century. The home of gipsies for most of the summer seasons, as well as for steam roundabouts, coconut shies, aunt sallies and shooting galleries, the greens were levelled and Pawley's Green, near the Kursaal, was paved and fenced, with gardens laid out, and a bandstand erected on it.

The western end of Marine Parade, a series of rather grand houses, beginning at the extreme western end in the bow-fronted house built in the late eighteenth century. The census of 1881, the approximate date of this photograph, indicates that these properties comprised mainly private houses, lodgings and shops, including the chemists of Charles King, 'Refreshment Rooms' and public houses. (*Reproduced by kind permission of Southend Museums*)

Just after the turn of the century there were many more refreshment rooms, restaurants and dining rooms, together with oyster bars and hotels, in response to the growing demand from trippers. Later, again in response to demand, many of these establishments were converted into amusement arcades (four in this small stretch by the 1970s), but still with a number of restaurants and hotels. (*Author*)

Marine Parade, or 'The Golden Mile', was originally a single-lane seafront road, giving access to shops, public houses and private residences. The principal access, until the early nineteenth century, was by Southend Lane, at the eastern end, the road now known as Southchurch Avenue. As the nineteenth century progressed the greens, which used to front the road on the beach side, were given over to side shows, stalls and fairground rides and amusements, cricket and temporary shops. In the late nineteenth century, when this photograph was taken, the greens had been confined to the eastern end of Marine Parade, and beyond, and the seafront given over to promenading. On the other side of the road, however, public houses and souvenir shops plied their trade, particularly to the day-trippers, those 'lower class of excursionists' so reviled by the town fathers, but who, they knew, were the principal mainstay of the economy of this part of town, at least. The Golden Mile it certainly was. (*From the Noakes Collection, reproduced by kind permission of John Kennedy Melling*)

Today the broad dual carriageway is still thronged in the summer months with crowds of day-trippers, but not in the same vast numbers as previously. Private houses are now converted to amusement arcades full of the shouts of bingo callers and the sounds of electronic games machines. This eastern part of the seafront is still very different from the west. (*Author*)

Looking eastwards along Marine Parade, *c.* 1897. Although we cannot be certain, it is likely that the flags are in celebration of Queen Victoria's Diamond Jubilee of that year. On the right is a water cart, with the words 'Corporation of Southend-on-Sea' on the back, an indication that the photograph was taken after the creation of the Municipal Borough in 1892. We can also see that the photograph predates the widening of the seafront road, at the beginning of the twentieth century. (*Reproduced by kind permission of Southend Museums*)

A similar view today, with permanent illuminations now replacing the flags. The road is now, of course, double the width of the original Marine Parade. On the right the tops of the large rides in 'Adventure Island' can just be seen. The road has for many years been known as Southend's 'Golden Mile', many of the private houses on the landward side now being amusement arcades. (*Author*)

An early postcard view of Marine Parade in about 1900, showing the west end of the Parade. A single carriageway was divided from the beach by a simple iron railing. This was the 'Lower Town' of Southend, that part to which the 'lower classes of excursionists' were confined, and where all their needs were met, according to the local Council, who wished to keep the western part of the seafront (west of the pier) for the 'better class' of visitor. So here, in the east, were the amusements, the shooting galleries, coconut shies and aunt sallies and, indeed, many of the shops and public houses. The shops included Luigi Offredi's refreshment rooms (at 25 Marine Parade) and at no. 43, the shop of Henry Thomas Dowsett, provision merchant. (*Reproduced by kind permission of Southend Museums*)

In 1902 the local Council put forward a scheme for widening Marine Parade and constructing an outer sea wall, involving reclaiming a large amount of the foreshore. 'It must be apparent to the most casual observer that at present there is absolutely no proper provision for the accommodation of the thousands of summer visitors who come to Southend in search of a pleasure ground.' (Council Minutes) (*Author*)

A late nineteenth-century view of the eastern end of Marine Parade. The beach slopes up to the 'greens' which, in turn, lead directly from the narrow seafront road. The water's edge is crowded with 'excursionists' as the newspapers liked to call them, together with the small rowing boats which were used for pleasure trips 'around the bay'. Towards the centre right you can make out the bandstand which became known, from the principal act appearing there, as the 'Jolly Boys'' bandstand. (*Reproduced by kind permission of Southend Museums*)

In the early twentieth century a number of improvements were effected, including the widening of the road and clearing away the greens. Here we see the same view today, with public conveniences occupying the site of the Jolly Boys' bandstand, while the greens have been concreted over. (*Author*)

Marine Parade, *c.* 1900. On the left is the Hope Hotel, built in about 1790, and further along is the Cornucopia public house. In the foreground are the horse-drawn charabancs which took passengers on rides to Shoebury and back. These may have been owned by the Triggs, who ran the Cornucopia public house. From the large number of such horse-drawn vehicles which plied their trade along this stretch of the seafront, it was also called the Cart Parade. (*Reproduced by kind permission of Southend Museums*)

The most immediate difference today is the fact that the road has been doubled in width. The seat in the top photograph would now be in the central reservation in the lower picture. The architecture has remained largely unaltered, except for the central group of buildings. (*Author*)

Probably the earliest known view of Marine Parade, dating to about 1880. Taken from the west, we can see the Falcon public house (originally a private house, 4 Strutts Parade) and, at the far end, the large and imposing Rayleigh House. At this time the whole of Marine Parade comprised private houses, lodging houses and pubs and shops. This particular stretch of the road was known as Strutts Parade after its builder, John James Strutt, second Baron Rayleigh. (*Reproduced by kind permission of Southend Museums*)

The Falcon has remained almost intact – although there have been many other changes. The large majority of premises are now given over to either amusements or food outlets. (*Author*)

This view of the Falcon Public House, along Marine Parade, also shows the premises of George Dawson, the photographer, which can be seen in the centre of the photograph, at 46 Marine Parade. Dawson, a chemist by trade, was a very good photographer in his own right and his chemist shop on the seafront sold photographic supplies to the amateur market. This shop was the first in Southend, it has been said, to have a plate-glass shop window installed, and was also the oldest established chemist business in the town, that trade having been carried on in these premises since at least 1852. (*Reproduced by kind permission of Southend Museums*)

Despite the change of use, from chemist to fish-and-chip shop, the architecture above ground-floor-level has remained virtually unaltered, as is the case with many of the buildings along Marine Parade. (*Author*)

Strutt's Parade, Marine Parade, from the east. The large house nearest the camera is Rayleigh House, the home of Major General William Goodday Strutt, a veteran of the Peninsula War, who moved to Southend in 1824. Strutt was a leading figure in local affairs, being involved both with the promotion of the building of Southend's first pier, and in the building of Southend's parish church, St John's. In 1871, only shortly before this photograph was taken, Rayleigh House was the home of Charles Ball and his wife. The Falcon public house can be seen towards the left of the picture. (*Reproduced by kind permission of Southend Museums*)

Although at first sight this section of Marine Parade may look very different today, above the ground-floor amusement arcades and shop frontages the early mid-nineteenth century architecture is still evident. The Falcon public house is instantly recognisable and even Rayleigh House, although much altered, is still identifiable. (*Author*)

The first brick cottages in 'South End' were constructed by John Remnant for the oyster fishermen in 1767. These were called Pleasant Row, and stood at the northern end of Pleasant Road. The earliest cartographic depiction of this road is in Chapman and André's *Atlas of Essex*, published in 1777. Before this time Southend comprised principally the farms and other timber buildings to the east of Southend Lane (now Southchurch Avenue and Old Southend Road), together with a few buildings along the seafront. (*Reproduced by kind permission of Southend Museums*)

These buildings were demolished in the mid-1950s, to be replaced by a block of modern houses and gardens; even the road was renamed. Now it is called Ash Walk, and there is no trace of Southend's first brick dwellings. (*Author*)

The Ship Hotel had been built by 1758, and was the home of Mr Hain until 1764 when it was converted into a hotel. It formed part of the early expansion of 'South End' from its origins in the small farming and fishing settlement to the east, along the seafront. This view, of 1908, shows queues of children waiting for the 'penny fund' dinner. In fact about 900 children attended the dinner, arranged annually by Mr G. Myall and other local businessmen for the poorer children of the borough. After the dinner each child received a piece of cake, a mince pie and a bag containing an orange, apple and some nuts. (*Reproduced by kind permission of Southend Museums*)

The old Ship was demolished in the 1950s, together with many of the other early buildings nearby. The pub was rebuilt on a rather smaller scale, and serves a very different public to that of the original building. (*Author*)

Grovesnor Place, seen here in about 1880, was a large block or terrace of houses in Marine Parade, between Pleasant Road and Southchurch Avenue, and just to the west of the Ship Hotel. In the *Guide to Southend* of 1824, it is stated that Grosvenor Place 'contains several good houses of different sizes, fitted up as lodgings'. In fact, this property comprised three main houses which in 1906, for example, were occupied by Mrs Trigg, Mrs Walker and Henry Barefoot. (*Reproduced by kind permission of Southend Museums*)

It is not known when Grosvenor Place was taken down (perhaps in the late 1930s, as it is still recorded in the 1935 street directory), but on its site is now the Happidrome amusement arcade. (*Author*)

The corner of Pleasant Road and Marine Parade is seen here in the early 1950s. This whole row, from here to the junction with Southchurch Avenue, has undergone drastic changes over the past fifty years. In the street directories for the early 1950s the corner premises were described as 'Shellfish bar', being little more than a front extension on what was originally a private house. In the earlier part of the twentieth century this had been a Methodist Mission home of rest. (*Reproduced by kind permission of Southend Borough Engineers Department*)

Like much of the seafront in earlier times, private houses and temporary structures have given way, as here, to cafés and amusement arcades – here the Orient Express and 'Happidrome'. It will probably be agreed that this is an improvement to the street frontage. (*Author*)

This row of brick cottages, of early nineteenth-century date, is on the corner of Marine Parade and Southchurch Avenue. Here, in the 1920s, can be seen the row of small shops – confectioners and shellfish stalls – which fronted the buildings. On the opposite side of the road, to the right, is the Kursaal. (*Reproduced by kind permission of Essex Record Office, D/BC 1/4/10/11/179*)

By about 1960 a few more – seafood – shops had opened. (*Reproduced by kind permission of Southend Borough Engineers Department*)

'Change' not 'progress' must be the kindest way to describe what has happened here. Replacing part of the history of the 'Lower' town of Southend is this hideous 'plastic' castle with fish-and-chip shops and amusements. The less said about this, the better. (*Author*)

Marine Parade from the east. The central point of this photograph is the Hope Hotel, built in about 1790, and the oldest surviving public house on the seafront road which, as can be seen, is a very narrow street. In the foreground are the greens on which, in the season, cricket matches used to be played in the early nineteenth century, and later in the century temporary amusement stalls were set up for the trippers. These amusements included steam roundabouts, shooting galleries, aunt sallies and so on, many of which caused residents to complain of the noise. (*Reproduced by kind permission of Southend Museums*)

The widening schemes of the early twentieth century disposed of the greens, resulting eventually in a dual carriageway road and sea wall defences. In recent years it has been necessary to install traffic bumps to prevent speeding along the seafront, which, it is interesting to note, was a complaint also of the later nineteenth century, but then applied to those 'furious donkey drivers'. (*Author*)

The Kursaal and Revolving Tower. This picture was probably taken very shortly after the opening of the Kursaal in 1901. In that year, also, it was proposed in Council that Pawley's Green should be improved, by being levelled, paved and planted with trees and shrubs and that an unclimbable fence should be erected around the green. Mr Page paid rent for stationing his bathing machines on the edge of the green. The Revolving Tower was opened in 1898, but was removed in 1905 following questions about its safety. (*Reproduced by kind permission of Southend Museums*)

The Kursaal expanded over the years to become the premier amusement park in the south of England. The green had been 'improved' in the early part of the twentieth century, and the bandstand which was erected in the middle of the green was made famous by the 'Jolly Boys'. Today there is no sign of bandstand or green; much of the area is now taken up by this car park and, further to the west, public conveniences. (*Author*)

Before the erection of the Kursaal buildings the corner of Southchurch Avenue (originally Southend Lane) and Eastern Esplanade was occupied by this small group of stalls and shops. Behind them, the Marine Park was to be laid out in the 1890s. (*Reproduced by kind permission of Southend Museums*)

The Kursaal was opened in 1901. These buildings stood at the south-west corner of the Marine Park, which had been laid out for Alfred and Bernard Wiltshire Tollhurst by H. Milner, a landscape designer, in 1894. Originally the park was to be simply that, with bandstage, walks, gardens, lake and so on, but shortly before its opening the owners were persuaded to include a small 4 acre annexe for amusements. This proved so successful that other areas of the park were leased out for the erection of rides, and in 1896 plans were drawn up for a grand brick entrance, with domes and large Blackpool-like tower. After several financial failures the brick entrance and other buildings were eventually completed, but the tower was never built. The name Kursaal was adopted from the company which successfully completed the project – the Margate and Southend Kursaals Ltd; it means a 'cure-all', presumably adapted to mean a place of healthy amusement. (*Reproduced by kind permission of Southend Museums*)

After several years of declining attendances, the park closed in 1973 and was given over to housing. The Kursaal buildings eventually closed in 1986. Following many years of proposed developments but neglect, the site was purchased by Southend Council and the dome was awarded a Grade II listed protection. The Rowallan Group redeveloped the site, which eventually re-opened as the Kursaal in 1998. (*Author*)

The helter skelter at Britannia Funfair. This stood for fifty years, having been erected in 1910 on the site of the old revolving tower, which had been removed in 1905. This very small funfair could never match the thrills and spills of the Kursaal, of course, and the helter skelter never attracted visitors in large numbers. (*Reproduced by kind permission of Southend Borough Engineers Department*)

The ride was never replaced, but some ground-level amusements – such as arcade machines – attracted the passing visitor. With the closure of the Kursaal in the early 1970s, fewer people looking for fun ventured beyond the end of Marine Parade. (*Author*)

A view of Prospect Place and Row, with the Castle public house to the right, *c.* 1900. These houses were built adjacent to the beach at the beginning of the nineteenth century. At that time there was no major seafront road through to Shoebury. The property nearest the sea was used in the early twentieth century as a refreshment stall, where you could hire your beach trays and purchase the necessary teas and Lyons ice-creams. (*Reproduced by kind permission of Southend Museums*)

By the middle of the twentieth century these properties had become rather run down and, following the disastrous floods of early 1953, the Council took the decision to raise the height of the sea wall and to demolish Prospect Place and Row. This allowed the development of a direct route to the east. These properties were demolished by the end of that year. (*Author*)

In 1908 the tramway system was extended along the seafront to Southchurch and then to Thorpe Bay. Here we see the tramlines being laid in the section between the Kursaal and the gas works. The gas works jetty can be seen in the background. A branch line was built on to the Corporation loading jetty. (*Reproduced by kind permission of Southend Museums*)

The trams were replaced by trolleybuses on this route in 1939, and the last trams were taken out of service in 1942. In the intervening years the gas works jetty has been removed and the old red brick offices (formerly a children's home) were replaced by a very large and imposing structure, which has become something of a landmark, or an eyesore, depending on your point of view. (*Author*)

This view of Eastern Esplanade is to the north of Fairhead's Green, and looking towards the east. On the right, in the distance, is the Free Methodist Chapel which by this date, 1924, had become a workshop for the foreshore department, who used the premises for painting deckchairs in the winter. In the far distance can just be made out the gas works jetty spanning the road. (*Reproduced by kind permission of Essex Record Office D/BC 1/4/10/6/180*)

Today, the green is a car park, used to a large extent by patrons of the Sealife Centre, which can just be seen through the trees on the right, partly occupying the site of the chapel. On the other side of the road, in the distance, can be seen the large white building which stands in the grounds of the old gasworks site. (*Author*)

A view from the border with Southchurch, looking towards the west. In the right foreground are the buildings of Prospect Row, and in front of them are the bathing machines, which were such a feature of all seaside watering places in the nineteenth century. There is no real division between the beach and the road. A loading jetty is in the middle distance, with the masts of Thames barges just the other side. (*Reproduced by kind permission of Southend Museums*)

Today the beach and sea are kept in their place by a low sea wall, and groynes help to maintain the sand on the beach; otherwise it would be swept away by the river. In the distance can be seen the buildings along Marine Parade with the cliffs beyond and to the left. Long gone are the bathing machines, the jetty and the barges. (*Author*)

This view of about 1900 shows the old Castle public house on the right, and to the left the Methodist Free Chapel. In the foreground two girls are enjoying a ride on the Southend donkeys, along one of the greens. The chapel had been built in 1861 for Michael Tomlin, an old Leigh fisherman who travelled over south-east Essex preaching the gospel, despite being virtually illiterate. (*Reproduced by kind permission of Southend Museums*)

From the 1930s until the building of the Sea Life Centre in the 1980s, this area had been the last surviving green. It was enclosed and became a children's playground, with swings, roundabouts and see-saw. When the new attraction was built, the fate of the playground was sealed; much of it became, as seen here, yet another car park. (*Author*)

The Castle public house, at the eastern end of Southend (Prittlewell parish), had been built by 1818, its first licensee being recorded in that year as Thomas Brown. In the late nineteenth century, following extensive alterations, the licensee, J.D. Robertson, advertised his house as 'facing the sea with every accommodation for beanfeasts and other excursionists, also good apartments'. (*Reproduced by kind permission of Southend Museums*)

The Castle was demolished at the end of 1924. This followed a move to improve the walkway along the seafront, the licensee of the time, Mr Emmons, agreeing with 'the public improvement that would be effected if the existing building on Marine Parade could be swept away'. (*Author*)

ACKNOWLEDGEMENTS

The compilation of such a work as this is not possible without the help of a considerable number of people. First, I would like to thank all those who have generously lent or donated photographs to the public collections which I have drawn on for this work. Second, I must thank several people or groups of people in particular.

My sincere thanks go to Sue Gough and her staff at the Southend Library local studies department, who have so patiently and kindly dealt with my constant enquiries. She, and they, have been of invaluable assistance. I must also express my gratitude to Julian Reid and his staff at the Southend branch of the Essex Record Office. All my researches and queries have been made so much easier with their professional help.

Finally, I would like to thank those individuals who have so kindly allowed me to reproduce their photographs here. They are Martin McNeill, on behalf of Echo Newspapers, Sue Gough on behalf of Southend Libraries, and Julian Reid on behalf of Essex Record Office, together with Mr Wren, John Kennedy Melling and Mrs Janet Purdy.

BRITAIN IN OLD PHOTOGRAPHS